Book Five
NURSERY RHYMES

Illustrated by David Crossley

Brown Watson
ENGLAND

HUMPTY DUMPTY

Humpty Dumpty sat on a wall,
Humpty Dumpty had a great fall.

All the King's horses
And all the King's men,
Couldn't put Humpty together again.

LITTLE BO-PEEP

Little Bo-Peep has lost her sheep,
And doesn't know where to find them;

Leave them alone,
And they'll come home,
Wagging their tails behind them.

HEY DIDDLE, DIDDLE

Hey diddle, diddle,
The cat and the fiddle,
The cow jumped over the moon.

The little dog laughed
To see such sport,
And the dish ran away with the spoon.

BAA, BAA, BLACK SHEEP

Baa, baa, black sheep,
Have you any wool?
Yes, sir, yes, sir,
Three bags full.

One for the master,
And one for the dame,
And one for the little boy
Who lives down the lane.

TOM THE PIPER'S SON

Tom, Tom, the piper's son,
Stole a pig and away did run;
The pig was eat,
And Tom was beat,
And Tom went howling
Down the street.

IT'S RAINING,
IT'S POURING

It's raining, it's pouring,
The old man is snoring.
He went to bed
And bumped his head,
And couldn't get up in the morning!

JACK SPRAT

Jack Sprat could eat no fat,
His wife could eat no lean,
And so between them both,
They licked the platter clean.

Jack ate all the lean,
Joan ate all the fat,
The bone they picked it clean,
Then gave it to the cat.

OLD KING COLE

Old King Cole was a merry old soul,
And a merry old soul was he;

He called for his pipe,
And he called for his bowl,
And he called for his fiddlers three.

THE NORTH WIND DOTH BLOW

The north wind doth blow,
And we shall have snow,
And what will poor robin do then,
Poor thing?

He'll sit in a barn,
And keep himself warm,
And hide his head under his wing,
Poor thing.

RUB-A-DUB-DUB

Rub-a-dub-dub,
Three men in a tub,
And who do you think they be?

The butcher, the baker,
The candlestick-maker,
And up they jump all three!

I HAD A LITTLE PONY

I had a little pony,
His name was Dapple Gray;
I lent him to a lady,
To ride a mile away.

She whipped him,
She slashed him,
She rode him through the mire;
I would not lend my pony now,
For all the lady's hire.

LONDON BRIDGE

London bridge is falling down,
Falling down, falling down,
London bridge is falling down,
My fair lady.

Build it up with wood and clay,
Wood and clay, wood and clay,
Build it up with wood and clay,
My fair lady.

I SEE THE MOON

I see the moon,
And the moon sees me.
God bless the moon,
And God bless me.

CLAP HANDS

Clap hands, clap hands,
'Til Daddy comes home.
He will bring goodies
For baby alone.

CHRISTMAS IS COMING

Christmas is coming,
The geese are getting fat,
Please to put a penny
In the old man's hat.

If you haven't got a penny,
A ha'penny will do;
If you haven't got a ha'penny,
Then God bless you.

ROSES ARE RED

Roses are red,
Violets are blue,
Sugar is sweet
And so are you.